MATT CHRISTOPHER®

At the Plate with . . .

Sammy Sosa

MATT CHRISTOPHER®

At the Plate with . . .
Sammy Sosa

Text by Glenn Stout

LITTLE, BROWN AND COMPANY
New York ✠ An AOL Time Warner Company

First Edition

Matt Christopher® is a registered trademark
of Catherine M. Christopher.

Library of Congress Cataloging-in-Publication Data

Stout, Glenn.
    At the plate with . . . Sammy Sosa / Glenn Stout.
        p.   cm.
    Summary: A biography of the Chicago Cubs power lifter, Sammy Sosa, from his poor childhood in the Dominican Republic to the home run record-breaking 1998 season.
    ISBN 0-316-13477-5
    1. Sosa, Sammy, 1968–   Juvenile literature.   2. Baseball players — Dominican Republic   Biography   Juvenile literature [1. Sosa, Sammy, 1968–   .   2. Baseball players.]   I. Title.
GV865.S59C57   1999
796.357092 — dc21
[B]   97-20562

10   9   8   7   6   5

COM-MO

Printed in the United States of America

Contents

MATT CHRISTOPHER®

At the Plate with . . .

Chapter One:
1968–1975

The Shoe Shine Boy

The Caribbean town of San Pedro de Macorís shares little in common with the American city of Chicago. The two places are as different as night and day.

San Pedro de Macorís is a port city of about 120,000 people in the Dominican Republic, which occupies the eastern two-thirds of the island of Hispaniola. The Dominican Republic is a poor, Spanish-speaking country. Warm sea breezes float through its narrow, winding city streets, where its inhabitants live in a jumble of buildings ranging from tin shacks and rattan huts to crumbling stone and concrete edifices that remain from an earlier age, when San Pedro de Macorís was once the cultural center of the Caribbean. Now, as then, the city is surrounded by fields of sugarcane, but much of the wealth that once came with sugar has disappeared. Many people in San Pedro de Macorís are poor, and it is common to see children as young as eight or nine years old shining shoes or selling fruit to earn a few pennies.

In contrast, Chicago is one of America's great cities, a huge commercial and financial center on the shores of Lake Michigan. Its skyline is marked by towering skyscrapers, and the sprawl of its neighborhoods and surrounding suburbs stretches for miles. The city is hot and humid in the summer, while in the winter icy blasts roar in off the lake and turn Chicago into an icebox.

Yet despite their many differences, Chicago and San Pedro de Macorís have one thing in common. San Pedro de Macorís native Sammy Sosa, outfielder for the Chicago Cubs, is a hero of, and at home in, both places. During the 1998 baseball season, his pursuit of history took baseball fans in both the Dominican Republic and the United States on an unforgettable ride.

Although Mark McGwire of the St. Louis Cardinals set a new major league record with 70 home runs in 1998, Sammy Sosa was a partner in his quest, hitting 66 homers and leading the Chicago Cubs into the postseason playoffs. Day after day, as McGwire and Sosa matched each other home run by home run, Sammy Sosa demonstrated that he is much more than one of the greatest hitters in the game of baseball today. He is also one of the greatest people in the game, and a man who is equally at home in the friendly confines of Wrigley Field as he is on the hardscrabble diamonds of San Pedro de Macorís. For not so long ago, Sammy Sosa was one of those young boys on the streets of San Pedro, shining shoes for pennies.

He was born in San Pedro de Macorís on November 12, 1968, the fifth of seven children born to Bautista and Lucrecia Montero. Bautista, who everyone knew as "Juan," was more fortunate than many of his countrymen since he had a steady job plowing fields.

Still, in a country where even today the average annual income is only about $1,000 per person, the Monteros were far from wealthy. Nevertheless Bautista and Lucrecia were able to support their children and make certain they were always clothed and fed.

They also kept close watch on their children. In

the Dominican Republic, poverty often drives some of the more desperate into a life of crime. The Monteros wanted more for their family and made certain to teach their children the difference between right and wrong.

The Dominican Republic has a long and rich baseball tradition. The game was brought there in the 1870s by Cubans who had learned baseball from American sailors. Like their Cuban counterparts, Dominicans immediately took to the game, and in a very short period of time, it became the most popular sport in the nation.

By the early 1900s there were professional teams. Many cities and towns had their own teams, and wealthy owners of factories and plantations began sponsoring teams as well.

Baseball flourished in the Dominican Republic as it did nowhere else in Latin America. By the 1930s Dominican baseball was so well established that teams began to raid the American Negro leagues of their best players, offering them more money to play ball in the Dominican than they could make playing in the United States. Dominican-born ballplayers were just as good as many of the American imports, and after Jackie Robinson broke the color barrier in the major leagues in 1947, major league scouts began visiting Latin America in search of ballplayers.

They found no richer ground than that of the Dominican Republic. Osvaldo "Ozzie" Virgil was the first Dominican native to play in the major leagues, discovered by the New York Giants after he had moved to Puerto Rico with his family. He made the major leagues in 1956. Dozens of other Dominicans soon followed Virgil to the United States to play professional baseball.

Although many such players were unable to overcome the cultural differences and language barrier in the United States and failed to reach the major leagues, some Dominican ballplayers became stars. Pitcher Juan Marichal was the first Dominican to become a big star. In a fifteen-year career beginning in 1960, he won 243 games, mostly for the San Francisco Giants. He won 20 games or more six times and made the National League All-Star team nine times. Other notable Dominican players include George Bell, who was named American League MVP in 1987 while playing for the Toronto Blue Jays, and

Joaquin Andujar, who twice won 20 games or more for the St. Louis Cardinals in the 1980s.

Both Bell and Andujar were natives of San Pedro de Macorís, which soon developed a reputation as a hotbed of baseball talent. Very few people in San Pedro de Macorís are wealthy. Of those that are, many are professional baseball players. When Sammy was growing up, Bell and Andujar were heroes in San Pedro de Macorís. They drove expensive cars and lived in big houses. Everyone looked up to them.

Sammy was still too young to know much about baseball. He spent most of his time either in school or helping his mother.

When Sammy was only seven years old, tragedy struck his family — his father died of a brain aneurysm. Suddenly, without warning, the family was plunged into poverty.

As a woman, Lucrecia didn't have the opportunities to work and earn as much money as her husband had. The only job she could find was working as a maid for a wealthy family. With seven mouths to feed, her small paycheck wasn't enough.

The family had to move into a tiny, two-room

house in a neighborhood known as Barrio Mexico, and everyone pitched in to try to earn money. That included seven-year-old Sammy.

He and his brothers tried to earn money any way they could. Sometimes they stood along the road with a bucket of soapy water and washed cars. Other times they sold fruit. But much of the boys' time was spent shining shoes.

They plied their trade outside factories and other places where people had good jobs, fighting for a place amid dozens of other boys trying to do the same. It was dirty, difficult work. Some days they earned nothing. What little money they did earn, they turned over to their mother.

There was little time left over for play. Although many Dominican boys spent their free time playing baseball in the streets and fields, Sammy had little time for the game. "I was never a fan," he remembers. "I never knew who this guy was or who that guy was. I was busy working, trying to make money for my mother."

One story illustrates just how poor the family was, and how hard Sammy had to work. It was Mother's Day, and young Sammy desperately wanted to buy his mother a gift. He stood all day in the hot sun, begging tourists for the opportunity to shine their shoes. But with dozens of boys trying to do the same, Sammy was unable to make any money. Finally, near the end of the day, a tourist handed Sammy a single penny.

He dashed off and bought his mother the only present he could afford — a single cigarette.

Another day, while out shining shoes, Sammy saw a wealthy American factory owner and his wife walking down the street. The woman was eating an apple.

He watched her take a bite, spit it out on the ground, and throw the rest of the apple into a garbage can. The apple was rotten.

Sammy raced to the can and picked the apple out of the garbage. When he noticed the two Americans watching him, Sammy became afraid. He did not want them to think he was stealing their apple.

So he asked if he could have the rest of the apple for his mother. "She is hungry," he explained.

The couple, Bill Chase and his wife, were impressed with the way the bright-eyed, dark-skinned boy had asked for the apple for his mother.

"My wife fell in love with him when she saw that," Chase remembered later. "We adopted Sammy right there."

From that day on, Chase looked for Sammy and his little brother José amid the hundreds of children who crowded around the factory each day begging him for the opportunity to shine his shoes. "I admired their work ethic," says Chase. "They were aggressive. They were the faces that were there every single day for two years. I always told them, *'No trabajo, no dinero.'* No work, no money. So they kept shining our shoes. They cracked from all the polish."

Sammy and his brother followed Chase everywhere. Every time Chase saw them, he let them shine his shoes and gave them some money. He wanted to teach Sammy the value of hard work; he knew that every penny was going home to Sammy's mother.

On the hardscrabble streets of San Pedro de Macorís, Sammy was a shoe shining all-star.

Chapter Two:
1976-1985

From Boxer to Ballplayer

The year Sammy's mother eventually remarried, Sammy adopted his stepfather's last name. Sammy Montero became Sammy Sosa. But his mother's marriage made little difference in the family's financial situation. They remained poor. After completing eighth grade, Sammy stopped going to school so he could work full time to try to help his family.

Yet every once in a while, Sammy would try to have fun like the other boys he knew. Most of the time they played sports.

Without any equipment or facilities, there were few sports they could play. They often boxed each other for fun, stuffing socks with paper for gloves, and dreamed about becoming professional boxers and earning fabulous amounts of money. One of Sammy's cousins, in fact, is a professional boxer today. But Sammy's mother didn't care for the sport. She worried that her son would get hurt.

Sammy also joined his brothers and other boys in the neighborhood in pickup games of baseball, the game everyone in the Dominican Republic loved. They didn't have any equipment, but that didn't stop them from playing.

For bats, the boys used tree branches or discarded pieces of wood. Baseballs were scraps of cloth wound with tape. For gloves, they used milk cartons. Many American baseball scouts believe that it is the lack of equipment, coupled with the intense desire born of poverty, that helps make Dominicans such good ballplayers. After hitting with sticks and fielding with milk cartons on gravel-strewn vacant lots, hitting with a real bat and fielding with a real glove is comparatively easy.

Sammy wasn't very good at first but he enjoyed playing. He couldn't help noticing that professional baseball players had more money than most Dominicans.

"I would see major league players from the Dominican, like Joaquin Andujar and George Bell," he once told a reporter. "They would build beautiful houses. I can remember thinking it would be nice to live like that."

On holidays such as Three Kings Day — a Dominican holiday held on January 6 with a tradition of gift giving — the young boys in San Pedro de Macorís would crowd around the homes of Bell and other stars. The ballplayers often handed out baseball gloves and other valued equipment.

Sammy hoped to get a glove someday, but he was never able to fight his way through the other boys. He made do with what he had.

When Sammy was fourteen years old, his older brother Luis watched him play. Luis had once hoped to play professional baseball himself, but the demands of working to support the family had made that impossible. Since he couldn't follow the dream himself, perhaps, he thought, Sammy could follow it for him.

Luis visited a man named Hector Peguero, who ran a baseball league in San Pedro de Macorís. When he was younger, Luis had played in Peguero's league for three seasons. Luis referred to the league as "the university of baseball." Dozens of players who had started with Peguero had gone on to sign professional contracts. Luis approached Peguero and told him he planned to work extra hours so his younger brother could play. He even promised to pay Peguero sixty-seven cents a week to give Sammy extra instruction.

Sammy jumped at the chance his brother offered him and worked out with Peguero every day. Bill Chase helped by buying him a baseball glove. Sammy took hours and hours of batting practice each morning with Peguero and the other students, hitting kernels of corn and bottle caps so they could make the few baseballs they had for batting practice last longer. In the afternoon, Sammy played on one of Peguero's teams. He was only fourteen years old, but baseball was already a full-time occupation.

Although Peguero wasn't initially impressed by his talent, he could not deny Sammy's desire. And ever so slowly, Sammy began to improve. He showed up every day, and never wanted to stop practicing. He was a fine natural athlete and was blessed with a particularly quick bat and strong throwing arm. He struck out a lot and often looked awkward, but when he did hit the ball, it usually went a long way. If Sammy continued to improve, Peguero knew he might stand a chance at catching the eye of an American scout.

American baseball scouts scour Latin America looking for talent. Not only are the players talented, but they are also cheaper to sign than Americans. A few thousand dollars seems like a fortune to a young Latin ballplayer. Latin American players are also exempt from the free agent draft and at age sixteen are eligible to sign with any team in baseball. As a result, scouts are always on the lookout for talented young players. Many major league teams have full-time scouts in the Dominican, and a few teams sponsor their own baseball camps and schools.

Most players are first scouted by what are known as "bird dogs" — unsalaried scouts who work for full-time scouts. When a bird dog recommends a player to a full-time scout and that player is signed to a contract, the bird dog earns a small sum of money.

Sammy was first scouted by a bird dog named Amado Dinzey, who worked for the Texas Rangers. He saw Sammy playing outfield for a local team shortly after Sammy turned sixteen. Dinzey thought the strong-armed player had potential.

But just as Dinzey began to take note of Sammy, so did other scouts. Dinzey didn't have the authority to sign players, so he contacted Omar Minaya, a former professional player who was a coach in the Rangers' farm system and also helped scout Latin American talent.

Minaya flew to the Dominican Republic to see Sammy play. But when he arrived, he learned that Sammy was in Santo Domingo, the capital of the country, working out at a camp sponsored by the Toronto Blue Jays. Several other teams had also contacted Sammy. Minaya didn't want the Blue Jays or anyone else to sign Sammy first.

Minaya contacted Sammy and arranged for him to travel to another city, Puerto Plata, so he could see Sammy for himself. Minaya met Sammy's bus when it arrived.

He could hardly believe his eyes. Sammy wore a ragged red baseball uniform full of holes and baseball shoes held together with tape. Although he stood five foot ten, he weighed less than 150 pounds. As Minaya later recalled, "he looked malnourished." Sammy Sosa didn't look like a prospect.

But Minaya hadn't traveled so far for nothing, so he worked Sammy out anyway, playing catch with him and watching him hit.

The more he watched, the more he saw to like in the young ballplayer. Although Sammy's arm was not very accurate, it was quite powerful. The ball darted through the air as if shot from a cannon.

But it was Sammy's bat that really got Minaya's attention. Although Sammy had an awkward, loopy swing, he generated tremendous bat speed. When he hit the ball, he hit it hard.

And like Peguero, Minaya was impressed by something more than Sammy's physical ability. "I sensed something inside him," Minaya later told a reporter, "a kind of fire. You could see he was hungry." Sammy approached baseball with the same determination he had demonstrated to Bill Chase as he pleaded with him to allow him to shine his shoes.

Minaya decided to sign Sammy to a contract immediately, before any other team came to the same conclusion. He returned with Sammy to San Pedro de Macorís and met with his family. He explained that he wanted to sign Sammy to a contract to play baseball in the United States and that, if he worked very, very hard, Sammy might someday play in the major leagues.

To Sammy, those words were like a dream. Many Dominicans fantasize about going to the United States, where they know it is much easier to earn a good living. Sammy was being offered an opportunity that very few Dominicans ever receive.

Then Minaya offered Sammy $3,000 to sign a contract, the standard bonus offered to all but a few Latin players at that time. Sammy said no. Minaya was surprised. Most Latin players are so eager to sign they jump at the first contract offer.

But Sammy was smarter than that. He realized that he could probably get Minaya to offer him more money.

Sammy was right. He asked for $4,000. Now it was Minaya's turn to say no. After a few minutes of negotiations, Sammy convinced Minaya to offer him another $500. Sammy agreed on a $3,500 bonus.

Although $500 isn't a great deal of money to many in the United States, the amount represented nearly six months' wages to Sammy and his family.

17

Sammy signed the contract on July 30, 1985. At age sixteen, when most American ballplayers are still in their junior year of high school, Sammy Sosa became a professional player. He was now property of the Texas Rangers.

But he didn't go to America immediately. The season was already over for the league they wanted him to start in. He would have to wait until after the first of the year to begin his professional career.

The next six months passed quickly as Sammy prepared to leave for the United States. Except for some spending money, he gave nearly all of his bonus money to his mother. He knew she needed it far more than he did. Besides, when he began playing baseball in the United States, he would earn several hundred dollars a month.

He bought himself only one gift. For as long as he could remember, he had dreamed of owning a bicycle. So he took a small portion of the bonus money and bought a bike.

Years before, another promising young prospect who had grown up in poverty also bought a bicycle after signing his first professional contract. He later became one of the greatest players in the history of the game, a person whose name became synonymous with the home run. His name was Babe Ruth.

Sammy Sosa didn't know it, but he and Babe Ruth would someday have more in common than a bicycle.

Chapter Three:

1986-1989

Minor Problems

Sammy Sosa's entire family accompanied him to the airport when it was time for his plane to leave for the United States. He was happy, but also sad to leave his family. When he looked at his mother and embraced her, neither could speak. Tears filled their eyes.

As the plane took off, Sammy looked down through the window as the Dominican Republic faded from view. He had no idea what to expect in the United States. Except for a few words, he knew no English, and he knew very little about the United States. At age seventeen, his entire family was depending upon him to succeed. He was more than a little afraid.

Sammy Sosa faced an uphill battle to reach his goal of becoming a major league baseball player.

Hundreds of young ballplayers are signed to professional contracts each year, but only a handful reach the major leagues.

For natives of Latin America, the odds are even worse. Not only must they adjust to playing against better competition, but at the same time they must adjust to an entirely new culture.

Until very recently, most major league organizations gave their young Latin ballplayers very little help in making that adjustment. Because Latin ballplayers are signed for so little money, few teams are willing to spend more money on these prospects in order to increase their odds of success. They'd rather spend their money on the big ticket prospects.

For this reason, when Sammy arrived in the United States, the Rangers organization had no program in place to help him learn the language. Sosa had to learn English from his teammates at the very same time he was learning how baseball was played at the professional level. Similarly, Sosa had to learn how to rent an apartment, go to the grocery store, order food in a restaurant, and pay his bills with little assistance.

Many Latin ballplayers fail to make the transition.

Despite their talent, they feel isolated and become homesick. Often, their play on the field suffers. As a result, many promising ballplayers have had their professional careers cut short.

If anything, Sammy Sosa was even less prepared for what awaited him in America than most Latin players. Only seventeen, he had to succeed in professional baseball at an age when most American players are still in high school. And he knew, from the very beginning, that the welfare of his family was almost fully dependent upon his performance.

The Rangers assigned Sammy Sosa to their minor league team in Sarasota, Florida, in the Gulf Coast Rookie League. Rookie leagues are for the youngest and most inexperienced professional players. As a player progresses, he can go on to play for teams in single-A, double-A, and triple-A minor leagues before reaching the majors.

But that doesn't mean rookie league ball is easy. On the contrary, it may well be the most difficult level in all of minor league baseball.

Most teams sign far more players each year than they have room for. In rookie leagues, individual players must succeed quickly and demonstrate that they are true prospects. If they don't, other players are waiting to take their place. Some players are released after only a few games. The pressure to perform is intense.

Sammy Sosa had one advantage. Omar Minaya, the man who had signed him to his contract, was the manager of the Gulf Coast team. He knew Sammy and wanted him to do well.

It also helped that the Rangers had a particularly good rookie league team that season, one with many other Caribbean players. Sammy's teammates included future major league players Kevin Brown, Juan Gonzales, Rey Sanchez, Wilson Alvarez, and Bill Haselman.

Sosa enjoyed his teammates and the opportunity to play baseball for a living. Although he struggled with the language, his teammates helped him and he didn't get discouraged.

He had an awful lot to learn about the game of baseball, however. Back in the Dominican Republic, he had simply swung the bat as hard as possible and hoped for the best. He hadn't paid very much attention to his defense or other aspects of the game. Most of his teammates knew the game far better than he did.

But Sammy's natural ability and enthusiasm made him stand out, even on a team with so many future stars. He hit .275, led the league with 19 doubles, and even hit four home runs. In comparison, Juan Gonzales, who has since become one of the best power hitters in baseball, hit only .240 with no home runs.

Eating nutritiously for the first time in his life, Sammy quickly began to fill out and show his true potential. Manager Minaya was surprised and delighted by Sammy's performance, especially his speed. When Sosa had first signed, he was considered slow. But by the end of the season, he was one of the fastest players on the team. He covered a lot of ground in the outfield, and his speed, combined with his strong arm, helped make up for his lack of knowledge about the game. It was still difficult to project Sosa's future performance, but he had played well enough for the Rangers to hang on to him.

In the off-season he returned home to the Dominican Republic, something he still does today. No matter what happens in his life, Sammy Sosa will always consider the Dominican Republic his home.

But he didn't spend the off-season resting. Because it stays warm all winter in the Dominican, Sosa was able to play baseball in the off-season, earning some extra money and improving his skills.

When he reported to spring training in 1987, he was bigger and stronger than ever. The Rangers were impressed, and he was promoted to their single-A affiliate in Gastonia, South Carolina, in the South Atlantic League. It would be a big test for the eighteen-year-old outfielder.

Despite being one of the youngest players in the league, Sosa was once again able to hold his own against older, more experienced players. He hit .279 and cracked 11 home runs with 59 RBIs. Juan Gonzales put up similar numbers, giving the Rangers two top-notch young prospects.

But Sosa still had plenty of room for improvement. He struck out nearly every game and made 17 errors in the outfield — primarily on throws — far too many for a professional player.

Still, in 1988 the Rangers promoted Sosa once

more, this time to their single-A team in Port Charlotte, Florida. Although still classified as an A league, the Florida State League is considered more competitive than the South Atlantic League. Only the best prospects get to play there.

Sosa's lack of experience began to show at Port Charlotte. Anxious to impress the Rangers with his bat, Sosa became increasingly undisciplined when faced with superior pitching. He tried to hit the ball a thousand feet every time he came to bat. He swung at a lot of bad pitches, and continued to strike out far too often.

There is a saying among baseball people about players from the Dominican Republic: "You don't walk off the island." This means players know they get the attention of scouts by hitting the ball hard and putting up impressive offensive numbers. As a result, their patience in waiting for a good pitch suffers.

That was precisely Sosa's problem. He rarely walked, and he showed little ability to work pitchers into what is known as a "hitter's count," where the pitcher is behind in the count and has to throw a good pitch. Sosa swung at everything. No matter what pitch they threw, or where, the pitchers usually stayed ahead of Sammy. And once he got behind in the count, he chased pitches far out of the strike zone and was easy to get out.

He finished the year batting only .229. Moreover, his power figures plummeted. His career was at a crossroads.

The Rangers were concerned about more than his play. Sosa sent at least half of every paycheck back home, while at the same time he tried to live the life he thought a professional ballplayer should. He wore heavy gold chains and dressed loudly. In short, he was living beyond his means. He got into debt, and the Rangers thought he was distracted by his off-field problems. They wondered whether their young prospect would ever demonstrate the discipline and dedication necessary to make it to the major leagues. In addition, his poor performance on the field had undermined his self-confidence.

Still, his potential was undeniable. Sosa now stood fully six feet tall and weighed nearly 200 pounds. He had blossomed into a player who at times displayed all five baseball "tools" — the ability to run, throw, field, hit, and hit with power. While few players ever demonstrate all these skills, the Rangers were not yet convinced that Sosa would ever harness his talent.

The 1989 season was a make-or-break year for Sosa. He had to keep progressing.

He got off to a quick start at spring training. Despite their misgivings, the Rangers promoted him once more, this time to their double-A team in Tulsa, Oklahoma.

Sosa responded to the challenge. He started off hot at the plate and stayed that way. Once he discovered he could hit double-A pitching, he began to relax and the rest of his game began to fall into place. He became a much better outfielder and showed more restraint on the base paths. He also began to demonstrate a grasp of how the game was supposed to be played on the professional level. Even if he didn't always succeed, he began to do the little things that help a team win, like moving runners up by hitting behind them or throwing the ball to the cutoff man.

By midseason, Sosa was clearly one of the best players in the league, hitting nearly .300 with 15 doubles, 31 RBIs, and seven home runs. He'd made only four errors and had stolen 16 bases.

In the meantime, the Texas Rangers also got off to a quick start, winning 17 of their first 22 games and dreaming of a division championship. But in May, the team slumped. By the middle of June, they were fighting to stay in the race.

Their problem was offense. At the beginning of the year, the team had scored runs in bunches, but as the season progressed, they had a hard time scoring. Several players had tried and failed to keep the starting job in right field, and the club needed some production from the position. They needed someone to jump-start their offense.

The Rangers looked to their minor league system for help. No one in the organization was playing better than Sammy Sosa. In mid-June, he heard what every minor league player dreams of. The Rangers wanted Sosa to join them.

Sammy Sosa was going to the big leagues.

Chapter Four:
1989-1991

Major League Challenge

Sosa could hardly believe his ears when Tulsa manager Tommy Thompson gave him the good news. As he later recalled, "It was the happiest day of my life."

His salary jumped immediately. Although he was making only the major league minimum, it was many times what he had been earning in the minor leagues. He would now make as much money in a month as he would in an entire season in the minor leagues. He began to dream about all the things he could do for his family, like build his mother a new house.

Sosa left immediately for New York City, where the Rangers were opening a series with the New York Yankees. In four short years he had come a long way.

Sosa looked around Yankee Stadium in wonder. In the Dominican Republic, the New York Yankees, baseball's most successful franchise, were well known. Their ballpark, Yankee Stadium, was one of the most storied fields in baseball. Hall-of-Famers like Babe Ruth, Joe DiMaggio, Mickey Mantle, and Reggie Jackson had all played there.

Ranger manager Bobby Valentine immediately thrust Sosa into the starting lineup, playing right field. He wasn't put off by the surroundings. Although the Rangers lost the game, 8–3, Sosa was impressive, banging out two base hits.

But even Sosa knew that life in the major leagues wouldn't always be so easy. It was intimidating to be on the Rangers. Pitcher Nolan Ryan was one of the all-time greats, and outfielder Ruben Sierra was an emerging star. In addition to suddenly rubbing elbows with these stars, Sammy was still struggling to adapt to American culture and hardly knew how to act or behave. Fortunately, some of the other Latin players on the Rangers, including second baseman Julio Franco, befriended him. Franco spent hours talking to the rookie about life in the major leagues.

In the four years he had been living in the United

States, Sosa had learned English, but he was still far from comfortable in the language and had little experience dealing with the press or fans. Talking with Franco and his other teammates kept Sosa from being overwhelmed.

One week after his debut, the Rangers traveled to Boston to play the Red Sox. In the second game of the series, the Rangers faced Boston ace Roger Clemens, one of the best pitchers in baseball. Three years before, in 1986, Clemens had set a record by striking out twenty batters in a single game.

But when Sosa stepped to the plate to face Clemens, he wasn't afraid. If there was one thing he was confident of, it was his ability to hit a fastball.

Clemens threw a pitch down the middle of the plate, and Sosa turned on the ball. It floated into left field, far above the famous "Green Monster," the tall left field wall at Fenway Park. As Sammy headed for first base, the Red Sox left fielder turned and looked over his head as the ball dropped over the wall.

Home run! Sammy raced around the bases, as happy as he had ever been in his life. He was beginning to feel like a true big leaguer. "From that day," he recalled later, "I said, 'I think I'll be a good player.'"

But word travels fast in the major leagues, and the opposition soon learned that while Sosa could hit a fastball, he would also chase pitches outside of the strike zone and could be easily fooled. He began seeing fewer fastballs and became overanxious. Instead of smacking base hits, Sosa began striking out. In the field, he started to make mistakes.

After Sosa had spent a little over a month in the major leagues, the Rangers abruptly decided that he was overmatched. In late July, they returned him to the minor leagues, sending him to their triple-A team in Oklahoma City. In 84 major league at bats, Sosa had hit only .238, with just one home run and three RBIs.

Sosa was terribly disappointed, and his disappointment showed when he reported to Oklahoma City. Instead of concentrating on his game and trying to prove the Rangers wrong, he brooded. In his first ten games with Oklahoma City, he collected only four hits.

The Rangers remained desperate to add punch to their lineup. They still felt they had a chance to win the division title, but decided that the only way to do that was to make a trade. The player they wanted was designated hitter Harold Baines of the Chicago White Sox, a very good hitter.

The White Sox, who had entered the season full of optimism, had collapsed and decided to rebuild. They told the Rangers that Baines was available, but at a price. They wanted some young prospects, and were particularly interested in Sammy Sosa. Although they knew he was still learning the game, their scouts had seen him play and believed he had potential.

The Rangers agreed to the deal. On July 29, they packaged Sosa with infielder Scott Fletcher and pitcher Wilson Alvarez and sent them to the White Sox for Baines and infielder Fred Manrique.

Sosa was shocked by the trade. He had never thought he would be traded, and the news brought tears to his eyes. Only six weeks earlier, he had had reason to believe he was one of the Rangers' top prospects and was happier than he had ever been in his life. Now he felt discarded.

The White Sox sent him to their triple-A team in Vancouver, Canada. But before Sosa began to play, White Sox general manager Larry Himes had a conversation with him. He assured Sammy that the

White Sox were excited about having him. Himes made Sosa feel wanted, telling him to forget about the last ten games. All he had to do was relax and let his natural talent take over.

Despite moving for the fourth time that season, Sosa felt renewed confidence. He attacked triple-A pitching, hitting .367 in his first thirteen games with Vancouver.

The White Sox had seen enough. On August 22, they called him up to the big leagues.

In his first game back in the majors, against Minnesota, Sosa was brilliant. He went three for three and scored two runs to pace the team to a 10–2 win, ending Chicago's three-game losing streak.

He remained in the lineup for the remainder of the season, playing center field, where he impressed observers with his instincts and solid play. At the end of the season the White Sox told Sammy he'd have a chance to make the starting lineup the following spring.

The White Sox kept their word. In the spring of 1990, at age twenty-one, Sammy Sosa won the starting right field job for the White Sox. He was one of the youngest players in the league.

But his promising performance over the last few weeks of the 1989 season created unrealistic expectations for his future performance. People forgot that he was still learning the game. Since he was replacing the popular Harold Baines, an All-Star, they expected Sosa to play just as well.

He just wasn't prepared to do that yet. He was playing regularly in the major leagues for the first time, and the entire season was one of adjustment for him. Pitchers throughout the American League learned how to pitch to the young prospect, just as he was learning to adjust to a steady diet of major league pitching. Sometimes Sosa won. But more often, pitchers gained the upper hand.

For much of the season, Sosa struggled. On occasion, he would display his obvious potential, cracking a long home run, making a great catch and throw in the outfield, or using his speed to swipe a base. Plays like these moved White Sox manager Jeff Torborg to call him "the best right fielder in the league," raising expectations even higher.

But at other times, Sosa seemed lost. He still showed little discipline at the plate, rarely walking, and striking out frequently. He made critical errors and sometimes took the White Sox out of big innings by being too aggressive, getting caught stealing, or trying to take an extra base at inopportune moments. The fans began to boo him, and the local media began to question the wisdom of the trade that brought him to Chicago in the first place.

Even Sosa became frustrated by his play. As a result, he'd try even harder and make more mistakes. As he later admitted, "I was trying to hit two home runs in every at bat."

Chicago chased Oakland for most of the season, eventually finishing nine games behind the first-place Athletics. White Sox fans were disappointed, and in the eyes of many fans, Sosa was one reason they failed to win the division. His lack of experience combined with his aggressiveness were interpreted as signs of selfishness. They thought he was concerned only about his statistics.

It didn't help that Sosa had contracted a case of "big league-itis." He was actually quite insecure, but he tried to hide his lack of confidence by acting the way he thought a big leaguer should act. His way of trying too hard, coupled with the language barrier, led many members of the media and even some members of the Chicago organization to view him as self-centered, more concerned about the way he looked and the clothes he wore than with the way he played.

He finished the season with a batting average of only .233. Although he hit 15 home runs and knocked in 70, he also struck out 150 times and made 13 errors.

In reality, Sosa was putting enormous pressure on himself to succeed. There was a great deal of money to be made in major league baseball, and Sammy desperately wanted to do all he could to help his family in the Dominican Republic.

In the spring of 1991, he retained his spot in the White Sox lineup. On opening day, Sosa seemed poised to fulfill his potential. In a tremendous performance in Baltimore, he cracked two long home runs and knocked in five.

But after his quick start, the same problems that had plagued him in 1990 reemerged. By midseason, he was mired in a terrible slump, hitting .200 with only a handful of home runs.

The White Sox ran out of patience. They sent Sosa back to Vancouver. They hoped the move back to the minors would shock him into playing better and help rebuild his confidence.

Sosa was crushed. His family had grown accustomed to the help his big league salary had been able to provide. Now that he was in the minor leagues again, his salary dropped dramatically, and he worried that he would be unable to fulfill the promises he had made to his family.

In Vancouver, he continued to play poorly. Despite this, the White Sox recalled him in September — but he played sparingly. It was clear that he was no longer in their plans.

Sosa was at a critical point in his career. Once a player gets the reputation of being a "triple-A" ballplayer, it's almost impossible to get back to the major leagues. This was happening to Sosa. He knew he would have to produce, and soon, or his major league career would come to an end.

Chapter Five:
1992–1997

From the White Sox to the Cubs

In the spring of 1992, the White Sox made it obvious that they weren't counting on Sammy Sosa. He hardly played during spring training as the White Sox evaluated their team.

The White Sox decided that they needed a more experienced player in the outfield. Coming to the conclusion that Sosa was too undisciplined, they simply didn't believe that he would ever make the adjustments necessary to become a valuable big league player.

The crosstown Chicago Cubs had just such a player. Outfielder George Bell, the Dominican native who had once been Sosa's hero, had come to the Cubs in 1991 after a stellar career with the Toronto Blue Jays, with whom he won the American League MVP award in 1987. Although Bell had played well for the Cubs in 1991, the club had finished below .500. The Cubs decided to rebuild with younger players and made Bell available for trade.

Former White Sox general manager Larry Himes was now with the Cubs. He remembered Sosa, and had been one of the few members of the White Sox front office who still thought Sammy Sosa could become a great player.

Himes thought Sosa might be a perfect fit on the Cubs. Their ballpark, Wrigley Field, was much smaller than Comiskey Park, the home of the White Sox. Himes believed that playing in Wrigley Field would help Sosa, both at the plate and in the field. It would be easier for him to hit home runs, and he wouldn't have to cover so much territory in the field. Both factors would help his confidence, which in turn would undoubtedly help his overall play.

The Cubs offered Bell to the White Sox, and on March 30, 1992, he was traded in exchange for Sosa and pitcher Ken Patterson.

Sosa didn't know what to expect when he joined the Cubs near the end of spring training. He was afraid that by joining the team so late, he wouldn't have a chance to earn a place in the lineup. He was surprised when the Cubs told him the starting job in right field was his.

Their faith in him gave Sosa a much needed confidence boost. For the first time since the 1989 season, he felt relaxed on the field.

The Cubs' coaching staff decided to start from scratch with Sosa. They realized that by moving around so much, he had never received consistent instruction. Instead of playing by instinct, Sosa was doing too much thinking, trying his best to please every coach. When he first came to the Cubs, for example, every time he made an out, the first thing he did was look to a coach for the criticism he had come to expect. He was expecting to fail.

The Cubs gave Sosa plenty of positive attention. They realized that he wasn't selfish, but had simply been rushed into the major leagues and lacked experience. They didn't blame Sosa for his failures. Instead, they tried to build on his strengths and work with him.

Cubs batting coach Billy Williams began to teach Sosa to hit to all fields. Before joining the Cubs, Sosa had a reputation for being a dead pull hitter. That's what he thought everyone wanted him to do. But

Williams, who had hit for both average and power for the Cubs, knew that in Wrigley Field, it wasn't necessary to pull the ball in order to hit a home run. If Sosa could learn to use the entire field, he'd get more hits and strike out less often.

Despite the fact that he got off to a slow start, the Cubs made good on their promise to Sosa and stuck with him. Ever so slowly, the lessons he was being taught began to take hold. His hitting improved, and he began to be more selective at the plate. And as he regained his confidence with the bat, he was less distracted in the outfield and his defensive play also began to improve.

In midseason, after being sidelined for a few weeks with a broken bone in his hand, he returned to the lineup and began playing like an All-Star. In Chicago, people were beginning to say that trading George Bell for Sammy Sosa was a steal — for the Cubs.

Sosa's hot streak pushed his average to the .260 mark. With two months left in the season, he was finally beginning to hit with some power. But just as he was finding his stride, fate intervened. During an at bat, he fouled a pitch off his left ankle and was forced to leave the game. Later, X-rays revealed a broken bone. His season was over.

Sosa was disappointed but determined not to let anything stop his progress. As soon as the ankle healed, he began playing winter baseball in the Dominican Republic and working out harder than he ever had in his life. He felt that he had made real progress in 1992, and he wanted to make sure he kept getting better.

In 1993, he did just that. He had overcome many of the cultural differences between life in the Dominican and in the United States. For the first time since coming to America, he was settled in one place. He began to feel at home in Chicago. The city was big enough that all kinds of people lived there, even other Dominicans.

He finally began fulfilling his potential. In one game alone, he collected six hits, and over the course of the season began to demonstrate the power that everyone in baseball thought he had. With 36 stolen bases to go with his 33 home runs and 17 runners thrown out from the outfield, Sosa was suddenly emerging as one of the most talented players in the game. Few players had ever hit more than 30 home runs and stolen 30 bases in the same season before.

After the season, Sosa splurged on a present for himself. He had a huge gold necklace made with a medallion that read "30-30," in reference to his home runs and stolen bases. Although Sosa was just commemorating a good season, the necklace made some people feel that he was concerned only with his own statistics. Such a display left a bad taste in their mouths.

Sammy rinsed that taste clean in the 1994 season with his continued good play. The Cubs were playing poorly, but Sosa was doing it all. With nearly two months left in the season, he was hitting .300 with 25 home runs. He appeared likely to finish the year with more home runs and RBIs than the previous year.

But once again, circumstances beyond his control stepped in. On August 11, the players, who had been playing without a contract since the beginning of the season, went on strike. They hoped that going on strike so close to the end of the season would force the owners to reach a settlement quickly.

Instead, both sides dug in and refused to budge.

Neither the players nor the owners trusted each other. In mid-September, the remainder of the season, including the playoffs and World Series, was canceled.

Baseball fans everywhere were upset. Many thought the players were greedy and concerned only about money. In Chicago, some members of the press cited Sosa's necklace as an example of the players' poor attitudes.

The strike wasn't settled until the following spring. When it was, the Cubs quickly signed Sosa to a new contract that rewarded him for his play. He signed a one-year deal for more than $4 million!

Finally, eight years after leaving the Dominican Republic, Sosa was able to take care of his family and not worry about money. He was set for life.

Sosa had gotten married several years before and settled down. He first met Sonia in 1990 at a disco in San Pedro de Macorís. He recognized the beautiful young girl from television, where she worked as a dancer on a variety show. He wrote a note to her and had a waiter deliver it. "If you will do the honor of having one dance with me, it will be the start of a beautiful friendship," read the note.

Sonia agreed. Although she found Sosa attractive, she wasn't overly impressed. He appeared too flamboyant. "I didn't even know he was a ballplayer," she later told a reporter. "I thought he was a traveling salesman in gold chains." But Sosa sent her tickets to a winter league game, and when the two began spending time together, she realized that beneath the flashy exterior, he was really very shy and goodhearted. When she turned eighteen years old, they married, and by 1994 already had two children, Keysha and Kenia. Since then, the Sosas have had two more children, Sammy Jr. and Michael.

The $4 million contract, plus the responsibilities of being a father, husband, and son, made Sosa even more serious about baseball. He began the 1995 season determined to have the best season of his career.

Due to the strike, the season got off to a late start. With only 144 games to play, major league players knew they would have to work hard to win back fans who had been put off by the strike.

The Cubs helped by jumping out to a fast start. With Sosa leading the way, Cubs fans looked forward to the club making it to the postseason. Baseball had realigned its divisions so that four teams from each league would qualify for the playoffs — the three division winners and a "wild card" team, the club with the next-best record. The Cubs, who hadn't won the World Series since 1908, had a real chance to go all the way.

But with the team's improved performance came increased expectations. Sosa was selected to appear in the All-Star game, yet some Chicago fans still thought he wasn't doing enough. Every time he struck out or made an error, he was booed. Some fans and members of the press even wanted the Cubs to trade him.

Sammy Sosa hadn't come this far in his baseball career to give up. Just as the team looked as if it was going to fall out of the race for the divisional title, Sosa took over.

From mid-August into early September he was spectacular, hitting home runs like never before and driving in runs in bunches. Over a span of twenty games, he hit 13 home runs and knocked in 32 runs, single-handedly keeping the Cubs in the race.

Yet even that wasn't quite enough. The club ran out of steam in the final weeks of the season and finished four games out of the wild card spot. But, for a while anyway, Sosa had silenced his critics. His 36 home runs, 119 RBIs, and 34 stolen bases in only a 144-game season more than satisfied the fans. No one spoke of Sosa in terms of his potential anymore. The Cubs rewarded him with a two-year contract worth $10 million.

He began the 1996 season by demonstrating that his performance in 1995 hadn't been a fluke. By the All-Star break, he was leading the league in home runs. It came as a surprise to many that National League All-Star manager Bobby Cox of the Atlanta Braves didn't pick Sosa for the team.

The reasons Sosa wasn't chosen are a bit hard to pin down. Part of it may have been that most Latin ballplayers, no matter how good they are, simply don't get as much publicity as American players. The language barrier plays a big role in that. Since English is usually a Latin player's second language, they don't feel very comfortable giving interviews, so they often aren't written about in the newspapers as much as American players with similar talents.

Another reason is the cultural differences between the United States and Latin America. Many

Americans don't understand Latin American culture. As a result, they misinterpret the behavior of many Latin ballplayers, and mistakenly think they are overly flamboyant, aloof, or undisciplined.

Sosa had been pegged as just such a player early in his career. But Sosa had matured and was feeling more secure. He had stopped wearing the big medallion and other large pieces of jewelry. Individual honors didn't mean nearly as much to him as his family and the performance of his team. He took the slight in stride and set out to show Cox what he had passed up. He did it the only way he knew how — on the baseball field.

In the weeks following the All-Star game, he was arguably the best player in baseball. He ended the month of July with a .358 batting average, 10 home runs, and 29 RBIs, earning him the National League Player of the Month award.

With six weeks remaining in the season, Sosa already had 40 home runs. He was on pace to hit 50 for the season, a figure that had only been reached nineteen times before. In the American League, first baseman Mark McGwire of Oakland was on a similar pace. As Sosa and every baseball fan in

America would discover in the near future, it would not be the first time Sosa and McGwire embarked down that path together.

Then misfortune struck. On August 20, as the Cubs hosted the Florida Marlins, Sosa stepped up to the plate against the Marlins hard-throwing pitcher Mark Hutton. With the bases loaded, Hutton tried to jam Sosa with a pitch inside. The ball tailed in and struck Sosa on the hand.

Although a run scored, giving Sosa his 100th RBI of the season, he was forced from the game. Cubs doctors X-rayed his hand and discovered it was broken. His season was over. He underwent an operation and as soon as his hand healed, began working out in anticipation of the 1997 season.

As had become his custom, Sosa returned to the Dominican Republic in the off-season. Now he was one of the players pursued by young Dominican boys who wanted to shine his shoes or pester him for baseball equipment.

It would have been easier for Sosa to stay away from the public. But he had not forgotten that not so long ago, he had been one of those boys himself. So, after making sure to take care of his family and building his mother the new home he had dreamed of so many years before, he spread his good fortune to the Dominican people. In the off-season, he donated more than $500,000 to charities.

Remembering how hard it had been to get baseball equipment and proper instruction when he was first learning the game, Sosa began work on a baseball complex for youth leagues in San Pedro de Macorís. But he didn't stop there. He met with the Dominican government to discuss other ways he could help. He purchased ambulances and made plans to purchase computers for Dominican schools. He also built a shopping plaza to help provide jobs. In the Dominican Republic, people began calling him "Sammy Claus."

He didn't ignore the people of Chicago, either. In his adopted home, he made hospital visits, donated money to worthy causes, and purchased blocks of tickets to Cubs games for underprivileged children.

Few people in Chicago were aware of precisely how much good Sosa was doing for his native and adopted countries. Unlike some other athletes, Sosa cared little about publicizing his efforts, and he made his charitable contributions without regard for the tax benefit such donations could provide. In fact, he was unaware that such gifts were even deductible until Bill Chase, with whom he remains close, told him. With Chase's help, Sosa created the Sammy Sosa Foundation to more efficiently manage his charitable work. Chase now operates the foundation for Sosa.

Sosa wasn't giving to charity for the publicity. He simply felt that he had the responsibility to do whatever he could to help those less fortunate. "I want to be known as a good person more than a baseball player," he said.

People around the country finally began giving Sosa some respect. He wasn't a secret anymore. He began to be talked about as one of the game's great power hitters, just a notch below sluggers like Ken Griffey Jr. and Mark McGwire. One sign of this newfound respect came during spring training. A reporter asked him if he thought he had a chance to hit 50 home runs. Sosa just smiled and said, "Why not sixty?"

But the Cubs were a troubled team in 1997. Although popular former All-Star second baseman Ryne Sandberg had returned after a two-year retirement, he was no longer the player he had once been. Apart from hard-hitting first baseman Mark Grace and Sosa, the Cubs' lineup inspired little fear in the opposition. And their pitching staff was barely adequate.

The team got off to an awful start. For the first two weeks of the season, no matter how hard they played, they just couldn't win. When the team hit, their pitching fell apart. When their pitching held up, they didn't hit.

They lost their first fourteen games, one of the worst starts in the history of baseball. It wasn't even May, and the Cubs were already out of the pennant race. With little to cheer for, many Cubs fans turned their attention to Sosa. He was about the only reason to come to the ballpark.

He tried hard, but with the team playing poorly, his game came under intense scrutiny. He still made many little mistakes, like getting thrown out trying to steal at a critical time in the game. Although such mistakes rarely caused the team to lose, in such a disappointing season, every mistake was magnified.

Apart from Grace and Sosa, no one in the Chicago

Competitors in the home run race, Sammy Sosa (66 HRs) and Mark McGwire (70 HRs) share a moment on the field before a game.

At a press conference before the Cubs play the Cardinals, home run record-chasers Sammy Sosa and Mark McGwire show that their competition is a friendly one.

A stellar outfielder, Sosa snags a foul ball off the wall.

Sosa acknowledges the cheers from the crowd after hitting home run number 60.

Sosa watches to see if the ball he just hit will clear the wall for home run number 62.

AP/Wide World Photos

Moments after hitting his 62nd homer, Sosa leaps in the air with joy.

Giving his signature salute to his mother (pounding his chest, blowing kisses, then pointing two fingers in the air), Sosa shares his 62nd home run with family and friends.

The Cubs show their appreciation for their star slugger and all-around champion player.

Sammy and his wife, Sonia, share a special moment during "Sammy Sosa Day" at Wrigley Field.

Known for his speed as well as his power hitting, Sosa takes off after his bat connects with the pitch.

Sammy Sosa's Career Highlights

1990:
Only player in American League to reach double figures in
  doubles (26), triples (10), homers (15), and steals (32)

1993:
First player in Cubs history to tally more than 30 home runs
  and 30 steals in one season

1994:
Won Cubs Triple Crown, with career-high average of .300, 25
  homers, and 70 RBI

1995:
Tallied more than 30 homers and 30 steals for the second time
Selected for the All-Star game
Named N.L. Player of the Week twice, the first Cub to do so
  since Bill Buckner in 1984

1996:
Finished injury-shortened season with 40 home runs

1997:
Became the first Cub to reach 100 RBIs in three consecutive
  seasons since Ernie Banks (1957–1960)

1998:
Finished the year with 66 homers, five more than the record
  set by Roger Maris in 1961, and only four homers behind the
  1998 record-breaker, Mark McGwire
Broke the Cubs two-year home run record, held by Hack
  Wilson in 1929–1930 (95 HRs), with 102
Named N.L. Most Valuable Player
Received 1998 Roberto Clemente Award, Major League
  Baseball's highest honor for outstanding service to the
  community

Sammy Sosa's Year-to-Year Stats

Year	Club	Avg.	Games	At Bats	Runs	Hits	2B	3B	HR	RBIs	SB
1986	Gulf Coast*	.275	61	229	38	63	19	1	4	28	11
1987	Gastonia*	.279	129	519	73	145	27	4	11	59	22
1988	Charlotte*	.229	131	507	70	116	13	12	9	51	42
1989	Tulsa*	.297	66	273	45	81	15	4	7	31	16
	Texas	.238	25	84	8	20	3	0	1	3	0
	Oklahoma City*	.103	10	39	2	4	2	0	0	3	4
	Vancouver*	.367	13	49	7	18	3	0	1	5	3
	WHITE SOX	.273	33	99	19	27	5	0	3	10	7
1990	WHITE SOX	.233	153	532	72	124	26	10	15	70	32
1991	Vancouver*	.267	32	116	19	31	7	2	3	19	9
	WHITE SOX	.203	116	316	39	64	10	1	10	33	13
1992	Iowa*	.316	5	19	3	6	2	0	0	1	5
	CUBS	.260	67	262	41	68	7	2	8	25	15
1993	CUBS	.261	159	598	92	156	25	5	33	93	36
1994	CUBS	.300	105	426	59	128	17	6	25	70	22
1995	CUBS	.268	144	564	89	151	17	3	36	119	34
1996	CUBS	.273	124	498	84	136	21	2	40	100	18
1997	CUBS	.251	162	642	90	161	31	4	36	119	22
1998	CUBS	.308	159	643	134	198	20	0	66	158	18
M.L. totals		.264	1247	4664	727	1233	182	33	273	800	217

*Minor league

lineup was hitting. Opposing pitchers were able to concentrate on the weaker hitters; as a result, Sammy saw few good pitches. Yet he didn't want to take a walk. He felt it was his responsibility to get the big hit. So he swung at a lot of bad pitches until he, too, began striking out more than ever.

He still had his share of home runs and RBIs, but his batting average plummeted. Cubs fans and members of the media thought he could be doing more. By midseason, with the club firmly entrenched in the cellar, some people began suggesting that the Cubs trade Sosa for some prospects and try to rebuild.

But Cubs general manager Ed Lynch, who had replaced Larry Himes, thought otherwise. He felt that the Cubs had several players in the minor leagues, such as nineteen-year-old pitching sensation Kerry Wood, who were very close to reaching the big leagues. With the addition of some veteran free agents, he thought the Cubs could be competitive in another year or two.

Instead of trading Sosa, he planned to build the club around him. So in midseason, when the criticism of Sosa was at its peak, he stunned everyone by giving Sosa a four-year contract worth over $40 million.

Lynch explained his strategy: "We see a five-tool player who is coming into the prime years, and who couldn't find the trainer's room because he's never hurt." Sosa's attitude was right, too. In such a dismal season, several Cubs players were constantly looking for excuses to get out of the lineup. But Sosa played every day and never complained.

Although Sosa was pleased with the new contract, it did little to silence his critics. They felt the Cubs were overpaying him, and cited the contract as an example of how baseball salaries had gotten out of hand.

If anything, the contract inspired Sosa to try even harder. But results were still hard to come by. In one incident, for example, he tried to steal a base at the wrong time, was thrown out easily, and killed what may have been a big rally.

Cubs manager Jim Riggleman knew he had to treat every player the same, even the big stars. When Sosa returned to the dugout, Riggleman yelled at him. His teammates and thousands of fans watching on television saw what the manager did. Many expected Sosa to blow up after the incident. After all, he was a big star worth millions of dollars.

But Sosa didn't. Although he didn't like being criticized in public, he realized he was wrong and accepted it.

Yet try as he might, Sosa was unable to salvage his season. Although he finished with 36 home runs and 119 RBIs, both club highs, he hit only .251, struck out 174 times, and had hit poorly in the clutch. At the same time, McGwire and Griffey both had spectacular seasons, hitting 58 and 56 home runs respectively. No one was comparing Sosa to Griffey and McGwire anymore. The Cubs finished the season with a dismal 68–94 record.

Although he was still a genuine star and one of the best players in the game, Sosa knew his career was at a crossroads again. No matter how many home runs he hit, he realized that all that really mattered was the score at the end of the game. None of his other accomplishments meant much if the Cubs didn't win.

Chapter Six:
1998

A Quiet Start

Ed Lynch knew that if the Cubs were to compete for the division title and the pennant, they needed some help. So in the off-season, he shored up the team's bullpen by signing star reliever Rod Beck, plugged some holes in the infield by acquiring Jeff Blauser and Mickey Morandini, and gave Sosa some protection in the lineup by trading for slugger Henry Rodriguez. Now opposing pitchers wouldn't be able to pitch around Sosa.

Lynch wasn't alone in his quest for improvement. Sammy Sosa decided he had to make some changes as well.

Cubs batting coach Jeff Pentland made some videotapes of other hitters and urged Sosa to study them in the off-season. He felt that one of the reasons Sosa struck out so much was that he was waiting too long to swing, then rushing. He told Sosa he needed to slow down and become more patient at the plate. He challenged him to work pitchers for 100 walks in 1998. If he did that, said Pentland, he could hit .300 and help the team far more than in the past.

Although some expected Sosa to take his ability for granted after signing the big contract, he surprised many by working even harder than before. He realized that with a big contract came an equal measure of responsibility, not only to his fans, but to his family and to fellow Dominicans as well. He knew that it was now possible for him to make an even greater impact on their lives. Sosa's apartment on the fifty-fifth floor of a Chicago skyscraper was not just home for Sammy, Sonia, and their four children, but to nearly a dozen other members of his extended family. "In the Dominican," he explained to a reporter, "the family, next to God, comes first, above all."

In the off-season, popular Chicago baseball broadcaster Harry Caray passed away. No one had wanted the Cubs to win more than Caray, and Sosa had been his particular favorite. Sammy was saddened when he learned of his death, yet it gave him one more reason to work harder than ever before. In his honor, the Cubs announced that they planned to wear a caricature of the broadcaster on their uniform sleeve.

When spring training began, Cubs fans were optimistic. They felt that the new players made them more competitive. But Sosa was still the key to the team's success.

He had worked out hard in the off-season and continued his hard work during spring training. With Pentland, he took hours of special batting practice, forcing himself to wait as Pentland lofted baseballs into the air, softball-style. He also dropped his hands a little lower and tried to keep his weight back so that at the beginning of his swing, his head was poised over his back foot. He tried even harder to go with the pitch, hitting balls on the outside part of the plate to right field. With his strength, and the relatively cozy dimensions of Wrigley Field, Sosa knew he didn't need to try pulling the ball so much, but it was hard to break old habits.

As the season began, Cubs fans became even more optimistic. The team played well in the spring, and rookie Kerry Wood, now twenty, appeared to have the makings of a dominant pitcher. Baseball experts concurred. Although few expected the Cubs to win their division or even qualify for a wild card berth in the playoffs, most believed a .500 record was a realistic expectation.

After their atrocious beginning in 1997, the 1998 Cubs were determined to get off to a quick start. After losing their first game, they won their next six and continued to play well for the first month of the season.

Yet hardly anyone noticed. Elsewhere, two big stories in baseball were capturing everyone's attention.

One big story was in St. Louis, where first baseman Mark McGwire was expected to mount a challenge to Roger Maris's record of 61 home runs in a season, set in 1961. Over the past several seasons, McGwire had emerged as one of the greatest home run hitters ever. In each of the past two seasons, he had hit more than 50 home runs.

His quest got an unexpected boost from the league itself. In 1998, major league baseball added two new teams, the Arizona Diamondbacks and the Tampa Bay Devil Rays. As a result, pitching talent was slightly diluted. Maris had taken advantage of a similar situation in 1961 to make his record assault.

McGwire got off to a huge start, homering in his first four games, and smacking 11 for the month of April. He was well ahead of the pace he needed for a new record.

The other big story was in New York. After stumbling the first week, the New York Yankees started playing fabulous baseball and were almost unbeatable. McGwire and the Yankees were getting all the attention of the press.

Sosa and the Cubs, in contrast, started off quietly. Sosa didn't even hit his first home run until April 4, and he finished the month with a modest total of six.

But there was no denying that he was playing well. His batting average was hovering around the .300 mark, and he was demonstrating much more patience at the plate. In Sosa's case, the fact that he wasn't getting much attention was good news — his critics had nothing to complain about.

The Cubs finally started getting some attention in early May, when rookie Wood turned in one of the greatest pitching performances in baseball history. On May 6, when he took the mound against the

Houston Astros, he was just another rookie filled with potential, just as Sosa had been years before. But when he walked off the mound three hours later, he was one of the most talked about players in the game.

Wood struck out twenty Astros, tying the major league record held by Roger Clemens. The Cubs won, 2–0, to improve their record to 17–15. With Wood anchoring their pitching staff, people around baseball began to talk about the Cubs as a possible contender for the NL Central Division title.

But they weren't talking about Sammy Sosa, and that was just fine with him. Over the past few seasons he had been the only story in Wrigley Field, and after each game, his locker had usually been surrounded by reporters. Now they were spread out all over the locker room, enabling Sosa to keep his focus. He went about his business, quietly putting together a nice season, a step up from his disappointing performance in 1997.

In mid-May, Mark McGwire went on a tear. After homering only twice over the first ten days of the month, he caught fire and by June 1 had hit an amazing 27 home runs. At that pace, McGwire wasn't just going to break Maris's record — he was going to shatter it. Every day it seemed as if the newspaper headlines brought news of yet another McGwire home run.

Sosa started heating up, too. On May 25, in Atlanta, he smacked two home runs, his tenth and eleventh of the season, each over 400 feet long. Then two days later, he did it again, and finished May with 13 home runs.

No one was putting Sosa in the same category as McGwire, or even Ken Griffey Jr., who already had 19 home runs. Yet in his own way, Sosa was fashioning a season that was just as good as those of McGwire and Griffey, hitting around .300, knocking in runs in bunches, playing solid defense, and running the bases smartly. Even better, the Cubs were still in the race for the division title with a record of 31–24. McGwire's Cardinals and Griffey's Mariners, despite being preseason favorites to win their divisions and having headlining stars, were off to poor starts.

But as May turned into June, Sosa and the Cubs, after a quiet start, would soon be making headlines of their own.

Chapter Seven:
1998

No June Swoon

On June 1 at Wrigley Field, the defending champion Florida Marlins played the Cubs. But the Marlins weren't nearly the same team that won the World Series in 1997. At the end of the season, their owner had traded most of their good players. The Marlins were now playing about the same way the Cubs had played in 1997.

Sosa provided evidence of just how far the Marlins had fallen and how much better the Cubs had become. For the third time in a week, he crushed two home runs, both more than 400 feet, and helped the Cubs beat the Marlins.

As Sosa's home runs began showing up on sports highlight shows around the country, baseball fans everywhere began to notice things that Cubs fans already knew. When Sosa hit a home run, he didn't stand at the plate and watch, or nonchalantly drop his bat and begin his home run trot. After making contact, he did a little skip and joyful hop as he watched the ball fly over the fence. Then after reaching the dugout, he would pound his chest over his heart, press two fingers of his right hand over his mouth, and blow kisses.

The hop and skip weren't planned — after taking a big swing, Sosa was a little out of balance and had to do something to remain upright. Besides, he was happy when he hit a home run, and it just seemed natural to him to jump for joy. And by pounding his chest and blowing kisses, he was simply signaling to his mother that he loved her and was thinking of her. By the end of the summer those two traits would become indelibly etched in the minds of every baseball fan in America.

Two days after he homered twice off the Marlins, Sosa hit another off 1997 World Series MVP Livan Hernandez. Two days later, the Cubs entertained the crosstown White Sox in interleague play. Sosa reminded his old team of their mistake in trading him as he homered in three consecutive games. The next day, he hit a fourth home run against the Minnesota Twins, giving him an amazing 11 home runs in only two weeks. McGwire had 29 home runs so far, but all of a sudden Sosa had 20. People began to whisper that Sosa appeared ready to give McGwire a run for the home run title and, perhaps, the record.

But Sosa had always been a streaky hitter, and when he failed to homer in the next five games and McGwire smacked two more, such talk soon dissipated. Everyone figured Sosa's streak was over and McGwire would soon pull far ahead.

Cubs fans were used to being cautious. Over the years they had grown accustomed to their team getting off to a great start, only to fall apart in the middle of the year. They even had a name for it: the "June swoon."

Sosa put their fears to rest. On June 13 in Philadelphia, he smacked home run number 21 off Mark Portugal, a magnificent shot to the opposite field. But it was two days later, when the Cubs played the Milwaukee Brewers, that Sosa gave a performance that screamed for attention.

Ace Cal Eldred was on the mound for the Brewers. Although he hadn't faced the slugger often, he had heard all about him from Brewers scouts. Eldred was cautious and respected Sosa's power, but he had confidence in his own ability. Since reaching the big leagues in 1991, he'd won more games for the Brewers than any other pitcher.

Sammy approached the plate for the first time in the first inning. Eldred didn't want to walk him, so he decided to challenge Sosa and take his chances.

That was a mistake. He threw a fastball over the middle of the plate.

In previous seasons, Sosa would have tried to turn on the ball and pull it down the left field line. As often as not, he would have either pulled the ball foul or swung under the pitch, popping it high into the air. But all the time he'd spent in the batting cage learning to go with the pitch was beginning to pay off. Sosa simply put the fat part of his bat on the ball and let his strength take over.

Crack! The ball left his bat in a blur and sailed high and deep just to the left of center field. It cleared the fence easily for a home run, landing over 420 feet from the plate. Chicago led, 1–0, and Sosa had home run number 22.

The fans at Wrigley Field cheered wildly. When

Sosa came to bat, they were beginning to expect home runs. They weren't going to be disappointed this game.

He came up to bat for the second time in the third inning. Eldred tried to be more careful. He wanted to keep the ball outside, where Sosa would have a more difficult time reaching it. But when the ball left Eldred's hand, it looked as big as a beach ball to Sosa. Once more Sosa went with the ball and drove it deep to the outfield.

Home run! For the second time, he'd smacked the ball over 400 feet.

Eldred managed to get Sosa out in his next at bat. But when Sosa came to bat once more in the seventh inning, the fans were already on their feet as he stepped into the batter's box. The game was on the line, and they were hoping their hero would come through again.

And he did.

Boom! For the third time that day, Sosa landed a pitch from Eldred over the fence for a solo home run.

As usual, Sosa ran around the bases quickly, almost as if he were embarrassed. Unlike many sluggers, he didn't try to show up the pitcher by jogging slowly, not even after his third home run of the day. Eldred simply watched him with a look of disbelief.

Sosa's home run spree gave him 24 for the season and pulled him into third place in the National League home run chase, behind McGwire, who still led with 31, and Atlanta first baseman Andres Galarraga, who had 25. But more important, the Cubs won the game, 6–5.

Sosa's hot streak definitely wasn't over. Two days later, he hit another home run off Brewers pitching. It was a monstrous 430-foot moon shot that cleared the left field bleachers in Wrigley Field, sailed over Waveland Avenue outside the park, and bounced off the roof of a building across the street.

Even Sosa's teammates were amazed. "I've seen a lot of his home runs," said veteran Mark Grace. "That's the longest one I've ever seen."

The amazing was becoming commonplace when Sosa was around. Two days later, against Philadelphia, Sosa smacked two more. The next day, he hit two again, and yet another the following day.

Sosa was smacking home runs the way most players hit singles. With less than half the season completed, he suddenly had 30 home runs, including an amazing total of 17 for the month of June alone. With nine days remaining in the month, Sosa was within a single home run of the all-time record for home runs hit in one month, set all the way back in 1937 by Rudy York of the Detroit Tigers.

Sosa's performance stunned the baseball world and pushed McGwire off the front page. Suddenly, it looked as if two players — Sosa and McGwire — would enter the last half of the season in pursuit of history. "Sammy's so hot I don't even have words to describe it," said Cubs manager Jim Riggleman. "He's setting standards I don't know if anyone's going to meet."

The national media turned their attention from McGwire and descended on Sosa. But he downplayed his chances of beating McGwire in the home run chase. "Mark McGwire is the man," said Sosa with admiration. "Everyone knows he's the man."

"Everything is going real well right now," he told the press. "I just have in my mind to go up there, make contact, and go to right field. Last year, I was in a situation where I was swinging at every pitch. This year I have a different attitude." He went on to explain that he wasn't thinking about setting any records, either for the month or for the season. The Cubs were fighting for the division lead, and he was simply trying to help them win games.

Maybe so, but his days in the spotlight were far from over. On June 23, he tied York's record with his 18th home run of the month. The next night, he made history.

The Cubs were in Detroit, playing the Tigers in another interleague contest. In the seventh inning, he came to the plate against pitcher Brian Moehler.

Sosa now approached each at bat the same way. As he stepped in, he thought only about making contact, about hitting the ball where it was pitched.

Moehler pitched carefully, but it didn't matter. He threw a ball outside, just off the plate.

Sosa waited on the ball . . . then exploded. He didn't try to pull the pitch, but hit it where it was thrown, to right field. The ball jumped off his bat and sailed toward right. The Tigers right fielder didn't even move.

The ball clattered into the seats far up in the upper deck, 400 feet away, for Sosa's 32nd home run of the season — and a record-breaking 19 for the month.

And it didn't stop there. On the last day of June, he set a new standard with home run number 20 for the month. In his last thirteen games, he had hit a remarkable 12 home runs!

But while Sosa was making headlines, Mark McGwire hadn't been silent. He'd kept up his record pace and still led Sosa by four home runs, with 37. Sosa was more than eager to give McGwire his due.

"He's still the man," he told the press again. "He's my idol." He continued to dismiss speculation that he might break Roger Maris's record. "No, no," he said, laughing. "That guy's a legend."

But all over America — indeed, all over the world — baseball fans were beginning to realize that in Chicago there was another legend in the making. And his name was Sammy Sosa.

Chapter Eight:
1998

Sammy and Mark

As June turned into July, Sosa looked forward to the All-Star game, scheduled to be played in Coors Field, in Denver, home of the Colorado Rockies. He was a shoo-in to make the squad, and he looked forward to both the game itself and the home run hitting contest scheduled to be held the day before. Already, people were anticipating an unforgettable competition between Sosa, McGwire, Griffey, Galarraga, and the game's other great sluggers. At no other time in baseball history had so many players reached the All-Star break with so many home runs.

But a few days before the game, Sosa began to feel pain in his shoulder. Team doctors examined him and although the injury wasn't serious, recommended that he sit out a few days. Without hesitation, Sosa announced he would miss the home run contest and the All-Star game, so he could rest his shoulder without missing any more regular season games than was absolutely necessary.

The Cubs, after all, were still in the most important race of all, the pennant race. They reached the break with a record of 48–39. Although they trailed the Houston Astros in the divisional race, they were in a strong position to make the playoffs as a wild card team. Sosa didn't want to play in the All-Star game if it meant aggravating his shoulder and damaging their chances.

Although he didn't play, Sosa still attended the festivities surrounding the All-Star game and cheered everyone during the home run contest, which was won by Ken Griffey Jr. His shoulder responded to the rest, and when the season resumed, Sosa was back in his familiar spot in right field and fourth in the Cubs batting order.

Already, in little more than half a season, he had put together a performance that most players would have been thrilled with for an entire season. In addition to his 33 home runs, he also had 81 RBIs, just a few behind McGwire.

But Sosa was most proud of two other statistics.

He was hitting .324, an improvement of more than seventy points from 1997, and he had thrown out more base runners than any other outfielder in the National League. He wasn't just hitting home runs — he was playing a complete game. Many members of the press credited him with being responsible for the Cubs' big turnaround and suggested that, even if McGwire set a new home run record, Sosa was on track to become the National League's Most Valuable Player.

Sosa quickly proved his first-half performance was no fluke, as did McGwire. Each player continued to hit home runs at a record pace, although McGwire continued to hold a slim lead over Sosa.

But the pressure on both players increased dramatically. Wherever they played, fans showed up at the ballpark hours before the game so they could watch the two players take batting practice. They cheered for each home run, but often booed when the sluggers failed to deliver. Both players were surrounded by hordes of reporters and hardly had a moment to themselves.

The two players reacted to the increased attention quite differently. McGwire, who had been under scrutiny since the beginning of the season, began to grouse about the attention. He complained that he was starting to feel like a "caged animal" and sometimes turned testy, responding curtly to questions from the press. At times, he didn't look like he was having much fun.

Sosa, on the other hand, appeared absolutely unaffected by all the extra attention. If anything, he seemed to enjoy it. Before each game, or afterward, he went out of his way to accommodate the press, and continued to laugh and joke with his teammates as if suddenly becoming one of the most famous athletes in baseball was the most natural thing in the world.

When the press asked him if he was feeling any pressure, he simply waved or shrugged and said, "Pressure is when you have to shine shoes. There are people with bigger problems than me. Believe me, I know." His difficult upbringing had given him a remarkable inner strength and sense of calm. Compared to what he had gone through as a child, chasing a record and being in a pennant race was fun, and facing the press day after day was nothing to complain about.

The more people learned about Sammy Sosa, the more impressed they became. He blasted away many of the stereotypes that people held about Latin ballplayers being selfish and standoffish. Over and over again, Sosa emphasized that he was far more interested in the pennant race than the home run chase.

Both he and McGwire ended the month of July still hitting home runs at a record-setting pace. Sosa had 42 and McGwire 45. Fans began to look forward to seeing the two players go head-to-head in August. Early in the month the Cubs were scheduled to play in St. Louis, while in midmonth the Cardinals would travel to Wrigley Field to play Chicago.

But before that happened, the two players suddenly found themselves in the midst of a controversy. A sportswriter discovered that McGwire, who is a fitness fanatic, was taking a substance known as androstenedione to help build his strength. Although the substance is legal, it is banned by many sports organizations because of questions over its safety.

Sosa was quickly drawn into the controversy. But he explained that he didn't use andro, as it is commonly called. Instead, he quipped, he used "Flint-stones vitamins."

"When you believe in God and you have a lot of ability and you're a strong person mentally, you don't need anything else to go out there and do your job," he added. Although some members of the media tried to get Sosa to criticize McGwire over his use of the substance, Sosa would have nothing to do with it. He continued to tell everyone he had nothing but respect for his fellow slugger.

The controversy seemed to affect McGwire. In the first week of August he failed to hit a home run. Sosa, meanwhile, continued to appear blissfully unaffected by anything. On August 5 he cracked home run number 43, and trailed McGwire by only two home runs when the Cubs traveled to St. Louis to play the Cardinals.

The press descended on Busch Stadium in droves. Interest in the series was high, and every game was televised to much of the country. Before the first game of the series, the contrast between the two players was dramatic. While McGwire appeared drawn and tired, Sosa was relaxed and happy.

Despite the crush of the press, the two had a

chance to meet and talk in private for a few moments. A friendly rivalry began to develop. Although the series wasn't quite as dramatic as many baseball fans had hoped it would be, on August 8 first Sosa, then McGwire, each smacked a home run, as if to reinforce the notion that they were in the race together.

Over the next week, the race for the home run title and the record drew closer. On August 10 in San Francisco, after striking out in his first two at bats, Sosa stepped up to the plate in the fifth inning against pitcher Russ Ortiz and belted a home run just over the reach of Giants left fielder Barry Bonds. The home run rattled the pitcher, and Mark Grace and Henry Rodriguez followed Sosa's blast with home runs of their own to put the Cubs ahead.

They led 6–5 with two outs in the seventh when Sosa came to bat again, this time facing reliever Chris Brock. Once more he got a pitch he liked, but this time he gave Bonds no chance to catch the ball. It landed far back in the left field stands, some 480 feet from home plate, to give the Cubs a 7–5 lead in the eventual 8–5 win. The two home runs, Sosa's 45th and 46th of the season, pulled him into a tie with McGwire.

Now Sosa began to receive almost as much attention as the Cardinals slugger. Yet he remained poised and self-controlled. After McGwire pulled ahead by hitting his 47th home run on August 11, Sosa responded by tying him again on August 16. "To tell the truth," he said, "I never think about a homer. I'm just thinking about the situation. When you're in the middle of a pennant race, you can't go up there thinking about home runs." The blast helped the Cubs to a 2–1 win, giving them a half-game lead in the race for the wild card spot in the playoffs.

Now the Cardinals traveled to Chicago to play the Cubs. With the home run race knotted, there were even more reporters on hand than the week before in St. Louis.

Sosa and McGwire were able to spend more time together. They met privately, and both players were pleased to discover they genuinely liked each other. It wasn't an act. Although each man wanted to set the record, both openly cheered for the other.

They seemed to realize that despite their outward differences, they had much in common. The home run chase had brought them together and challenged each one, not just to become a better player, but to become a better person. Neither seemed to notice their differences in race, language, or nationality. It was baseball that brought them both together, just as the game was bringing fans of all backgrounds together to enjoy the home run chase.

When the two players reached the field, the press descended on them, wanting to know what they had talked about. The two reacted like old friends. Sosa's cheerful demeanor seemed to have made an impression on McGwire. When he saw how much Sosa was enjoying the attention, McGwire seemed to relax as well.

Sosa joked that they had become so close "we are going to retire together." Both players realized they weren't in competition with each other, but with history. Sosa urged McGwire "to relax more at the plate," and McGwire later admitted that Sosa made him realize that "Hey, this game is fun. This is a game we love to play."

Fans everywhere began to fall in love with the two stars who suddenly seemed so down-to-earth. They were doing remarkable things on the baseball field, but off the field, each seemed to have their accomplishments in perspective. Since the strike in 1994, baseball had suffered from an image problem, one that had caused many fans to turn away from the game. All by themselves, Sosa and McGwire were bringing people back.

Neither man disappointed their fans when the two clubs met on the field. In the fifth inning, Sosa delighted the home crowd by cracking a home run off Cardinals pitcher Kent Bottenfield. The crowd at Wrigley Field went crazy, chanting, "MVP! MVP!" For the first time all year, Sammy Sosa led Mark McGwire in the home run chase.

But McGwire proved to be a tough competitor. In the eighth inning, he came to bat and cracked his 48th home run to tie Sosa. The game entered extra innings. In the tenth, McGwire won the game for St. Louis and took the lead by hitting his 49th home run.

Six weeks remained in the season. The new record was almost in sight.

Chapter Nine:
1998

Down the Stretch

A suddenly relaxed Mark McGwire left Chicago and went on a home run tear, racking up two more home runs in New York against the Mets and padding his lead. But Sosa refused to fold.

It seemed that every time McGwire hit a home run, Sosa responded. Yet each time Sosa pulled back to within a home run or two, McGwire pulled ahead again. On August 23, Sosa hit two long home runs off Astros pitcher Jose Lima, his 50th and 51st of the season, making him one of only a few players ever to hit 50 home runs in a season.

All over the country, the first thing baseball fans did when they opened the newspaper or turned on the news was to check if either Sosa or McGwire had homered. The situation the two players faced on the field, however, was quite different. The Cardinals were out of the pennant race, and McGwire could focus on just hitting home runs. But opposing pitchers didn't have to pitch well to him. If they walked McGwire, they didn't have to worry much about its impact on the game.

But with the Cubs still in the playoff hunt, every at bat was important. Sosa couldn't swing for the fences every time. Sometimes he had to cut down on his swing to move runners around the bases or just try for a base hit to keep a rally going. But at the same time, he generally got more pitches to hit than McGwire. No pitcher wanted to walk Sosa and have it affect the outcome of the season.

On the last day of August, Sosa trailed McGwire by a single home run as the Cubs played host to the Cincinnati Reds. In the third inning, he launched a two-run homer to help the Cubs to a 5–4 win. Entering September, both men had 55 home runs.

With a month left in the season, it seemed obvious that each could break Maris's mark of 61. But at the same time, both players were entering uncharted territory. There was more pressure on them than ever before.

Sosa wasn't worried. He just kept trying to stay focused on the pennant race. He knew that if he tried to help the Cubs win, the home runs would come. And if they didn't, that was fine with him, as long as Chicago kept winning.

"A lot of people have been telling me about the pressure," he said. "I know what to do. I am a grown man. I have been doing this a long time. Pressure was when I was back home and trying to make it to the United States." Playing baseball for a living and hitting home runs was, in contrast, fun. "There are people with bigger problems than me," he kept reminding people.

Even when Sosa didn't hit a home run, he was still helping the Cubs win. It was as if his performance at the plate had elevated his entire game. He was playing great defense, and the opposition knew that it was fatal to test his powerful throwing arm. And on the base paths, he was running with controlled abandon, taking the extra base or stealing when he knew it would help his team, not worrying for an instant about the possibility of getting hurt.

McGwire pulled ahead again. Then the Cubs traveled to St. Louis once more. McGwire had 60 home runs, while Sosa had 58. Fans all around the country sensed that the record would be broken during this important series. The only question was which player would hit numbers 61 and 62 first. McGwire was closest, but Sosa was just behind.

Major league baseball and the Cardinals anticipated a new home run record. Baseball dignitaries from all over the country came to St. Louis for the games. Although Roger Maris had long since passed away, his children were invited to attend the series.

In anticipation of the record-setting hit, major league baseball and the Cardinals made some special arrangements. The record-tying and record-setting home run balls were certain to become valuable memorabilia, so the baseballs used in the game were specially marked so they could be identified. And major league officials planned to hold a special ceremony after the record hit. Everything was in place.

Before the first game of the series, on September 7, 1998, Sosa and McGwire held a joint press conference. It was the first time they had appeared together anywhere but on the baseball field. Neither player gave any indication of collapsing under the pressure. Instead, they handled themselves like an old vaudeville comedy duo.

As the press deluged them with serious questions, they responded with a series of lighthearted answers. Since Sosa was always telling the press that McGwire was "the man," a reporter asked the two which of them was really "the man."

For a moment, the question appeared to catch the two players off guard. The last thing they wanted was a controversy of any kind. For a second, McGwire groped for words.

Then Sosa took over. He smiled broadly, grabbed the microphone, pointed at McGwire and quipped, "He is the Man in the United States. I am the Man in the Dominican Republic."

The room exploded in laughter. Both men beamed at each other and put an arm around the other's shoulders.

Near the end of the press conference, someone asked the two men who would end the year with the most home runs.

This time McGwire jumped in with the answer. Looking slyly over to Sosa, he replied, "Wouldn't it be great if we tied?" Sosa nodded in agreement.

Then both players took to the field to get ready for the game. As had become customary, the St. Louis crowd cheered every swing McGwire took during batting practice. Yet when Sosa stepped in, the cheering continued just as loudly. Everyone seemed to realize that no matter who got the record first, history might be made before their eyes during this game.

As visitors, the Cubs came to bat first. When Sammy Sosa got to the plate, he received a standing ovation. But he popped up to McGwire at first base to end the inning.

Then the Cardinals came to bat. Scheduled to hit third, McGwire swung the bat nervously in the on-deck circle for a moment, then stepped up to the plate after the first two batters were retired.

Cubs pitcher Mike Morgan was determined to pitch McGwire tough. Every game and every run was important to Chicago's chances to make the playoffs.

Then *Boom!* McGwire got hold of a pitch and drove it high and deep toward left field.

McGwire knew it was gone the moment he hit it. Home run number 61! As McGwire toured the bases, even the Cubs players slapped him on the back. In right field Sammy Sosa applauded into his mitt.

The game was held up for several minutes as a celebration took place around home plate and the crowd cheered. At one point McGwire turned to right field, pointed to Sosa and imitated Sosa's trademark pounding of the chest. Sosa applauded again.

Then the game resumed. The fans at Busch Stadium hoped McGwire would hit number 62 later in the game, but he failed to do so. Sosa didn't homer either, and the Cubs lost, 3–2. But now everyone in America wanted to be at the game the following evening, September 8, 1998.

The Fox television network even preempted their regular programming to show the game to the entire country. Millions of people stayed home that night to watch Mark McGwire and Sammy Sosa.

Anticipation was high and the tension almost unbearable as the game progressed. Neither player homered in their first at bat, but in the fourth inning, McGwire got a pitch he liked from Steve Trachsel. With a mighty swing, he drove it on a line toward left field.

Home run number 62! Mark McGwire had broken the record!

Once more, he was congratulated by the Cubs

players as he toured the bases. Sammy Sosa dropped his glove and applauded loudly. The stands were in an uproar, and the cheers of the crowd could be heard throughout downtown St. Louis.

After McGwire reached home plate, Sosa ran in from right field to show his respect for his friend, the new home run champion. When he reached McGwire, the Cardinals slugger grinned and lifted him into the air in a big bear hug. When he set Sosa down, the two high fived and playfully punched each other in the stomach, McGwire's trademark gesture of celebration. Then McGwire pounded his chest and blew a kiss with two fingers, Sosa's signature. The two men hugged again, and as they did, Sosa yelled into McGwire's ear, "Now you can go home, relax, and wait for me. Don't get too far ahead — I'll be there soon." McGwire just grinned.

The record was McGwire's for the moment anyway. Chicago lost the game, 6–3. But the season wasn't over. Sosa was happy for McGwire, but he and the Cubs had more to accomplish.

Chapter Ten:
1998

Sixty-two for Sammy, Too

Neither player homered over the next few days as
each experienced something of a letdown. But the
pennant race soon pulled Sosa back into the hunt.
While McGwire went homerless, Sosa cracked numbers 59 and 60 on consecutive days. Now he, too,
had Maris's record in his sights.

It set up an interesting situation. Although Mc-
Gwire broke the record first, it was beginning to
look as though Sosa might end up with the all-time
record. Fans everywhere still followed each player
closely.

On Sunday, September 13, the Milwaukee Brewers played the Cubs at Wrigley Field. The game was
very important to the Cubs. With only two weeks
left in the season, they were just hanging on to their

lead in the wild card race. They needed to win as many games as possible.

More than forty thousand fans packed Wrigley Field, the largest crowd of the season, to see the game. The game turned into a slugfest as players from both teams battered a series of pitchers.

In the fifth inning, Sosa came to bat against pitcher Bronswell Patrick. With one strike on him, Sosa told himself to swing easy and just make good contact.

The pitch floated over the middle of the plate. He swung hard.

Crack! The ball darted high into the sky over left field. As the crowd in the bleachers cheered and waved their hands, it sailed beyond them, out of the ballpark, and onto Waveland Avenue outside the park, where hundreds of fans had gathered, hoping to catch the historic blast. It disappeared into a mob of fans as Sosa circled the bases. He was one home run away from tying McGwire.

The game remained close. Entering the ninth inning, the Cubs trailed 10–8. But Sosa still had another at bat. Big reliever Eric Plunk stood on the mound for the Brewers. He was a fastball pitcher and didn't want to walk Sosa in such a close game. He decided to challenge him. Sosa was up for the challenge.

He met the ball squarely and it took off. Sosa took a little hop and skip as he left the batter's box, announcing to the world that he, too, had just set a new home run record. The ball traveled a path identical to his earlier blast, clearing the bleachers and crashing into the crowd on Waveland Avenue.

When he reached home plate, he was surrounded by his teammates and took several curtain calls as the crowd cheered for a full four minutes. Bleacher fans littered the field with paper cups and confetti. Sosa turned to a TV camera, pounded his chest, and blew kisses to his mother. There were tears in his eyes.

But unlike the scene at Busch Stadium when McGwire broke the record, there was no big ceremony at Wrigley Field. Sosa had caught major league baseball unaware, and besides, the game was important to the pennant race. Sosa's blast had pulled the Cubs to within one run of the Brewers. The record was great, but the Cubs needed to win the game!

They came back to tie the score, sending the game into extra innings. Then in the tenth, Sosa stepped into the on-deck circle with the score still tied 10–10.

It was like a scene from a movie. If Sosa could hit a home run, he would set a new record, take the lead from McGwire, and win the game, all in one swing.

But Cubs batter Mark Grace, hitting ahead of Sosa, had his own ideas. He smacked a home run before Sosa could come to bat, winning the game, 11–10. Sosa didn't care. The victory was all that mattered.

At a press conference after the game, he finally allowed himself to speak about the record.

"For the first time, I was so emotional," he said. "Today, number 61 reminded me a lot of Mark McGwire in St. Louis. When I got 62, it was something unbelievable. I can't believe what I'm doing."

When someone asked him how it felt to be grouped with the greatest sluggers in baseball history, Sosa shook his head. "Babe Ruth was one of the greatest guys to play baseball. Babe Ruth is still alive. Everybody remembers Babe Ruth like it was yesterday. I feel great to be there with Babe Ruth, Roger Maris, and Mark McGwire. But," he reminded everyone, "I've still got a job to do. I have a feeling we're going to make the playoffs."

Then someone asked him if he had a message for McGwire. Remembering how kind McGwire had been to him, Sosa said, "Mark, you know I love you. I wish you could be here with me today." The way things were going, it appeared as if McGwire's prediction at the press conference weeks before might just come true. Perhaps the two players would end the season tied after all.

Chapter Eleven:
1998

How Many?

The two players continued to capture the imagination of the sporting world. Now people who weren't even baseball fans couldn't help but follow the exploits of McGwire and Sosa. Two days after Sosa's record-tying blast, McGwire regained the lead by hitting home run number 63. But the next day belonged to Sosa.

The Cubs were in San Diego, playing the Western Division leading San Diego Padres, who many considered the best team in the National League. The Cubs needed every win they could get.

In the seventh inning, the Padres led 2–0. The Cubs loaded the bases and Sosa stepped to the plate. He pulled a vicious double down the left field line to score two runs and tie the game. Now the Cubs had a chance to win.

In the top of the eighth, Chicago loaded the bases once more. Again Sammy Sosa stepped to the plate.

Padres pitcher Brian Boehringer was in a tough spot. He had to pitch to Sosa. If he walked him, the Cubs would take the lead.

Sammy looked at the first pitch, but he didn't let Boehringer's second delivery get past him. He jumped on the pitch, and it rocketed into the second deck in left field. Grand slam! The Cubs led 6–2, and Sosa was again tied with McGwire!

Chicago held on for the win, and it looked as if the Cubs were ready to surge into the playoffs. But all of a sudden, Sosa went into a slump.

No matter how hard he tried, he couldn't get a hit. He even went hitless on Sammy Sosa Day at Wrigley Field on September 20. Perhaps, some people wondered, the pressure had finally gotten to him. Meanwhile, McGwire hit home runs number 64 and 65.

Then Sosa received some frightening news. Hurricane Georges, a monstrous storm in the Caribbean, had made a direct hit on the Dominican Republic. Nearly three hundred people were killed, and many thousands more were injured or left homeless.

Communications were knocked out, and for a long time Sosa didn't know if all his friends and family members were safe.

His slump reached twenty-one at bats when the Cubs traveled to Milwaukee on September 23. With so many distractions, few expected Sosa to break out of it.

But Sosa proved he was a special player. Somehow, he was able to focus on his task. He hit not one, but two home runs, tying McGwire again with 65 home runs. More importantly, his blasts gave the Cubs an apparently insurmountable 7–0 lead over the Brewers.

Yet no lead is ever safe in baseball. The Brewers clawed back to tie the game, and when outfielder Brant Brown dropped a fly ball in the final inning, the Cubs lost, 8–7. They were now in danger of missing the playoffs. They had to start winning.

On September 25, Sosa proved that his slump was over. He cracked home run number 66 in Houston, a tremendous blast of almost 500 feet, to again wrest the lead from McGwire. Then, forty-five minutes later, McGwire tied him again. But the bigger disappointment was that the Cubs lost.

With only two games left in the season, the Cubs were tied with the Mets and Giants for the wild card spot in the playoffs. The home run race was the last thing on Sosa's mind. He just wanted to win.

He showed that he was more than a one-dimensional player those final two days. Although McGwire cracked four home runs to finish with 70 and win the home run title, Sosa banged out two hits in each of the last two games, which the Cubs split. Although McGwire had the record, the Cubs were still alive. They finished the season knotted with the Giants for the wild card spot, and had to play a one-game playoff for the final spot in the postseason.

There was still an outside chance that Sosa could catch McGwire. The single-game playoff was considered part of the regular season. If he hit a home run, or two or three or four, it would count toward his season total.

The game was broadcast nationally, giving fans at least one more chance to see Sosa play. Although he didn't set a record, baseball fans everywhere witnessed why many people considered him the MVP of the National League.

In the Cubs' 5–3 victory, Sosa simply played a

quiet, steady game that helped his team win. He made every play in the field and had two hits, including a key single in the seventh inning.

After the game, he said, "This is where I wanted to be all along. This is great." While others were focusing on the records, Sosa was already looking ahead to the playoffs.

But it was asking too much of the Cubs, and Sammy Sosa, to defeat the Eastern Division winners, the Atlanta Braves, in the first round of the playoffs. The Cubs pitching staff was exhausted, a matter that had been made worse by the loss of pitcher Kerry Wood to injury. Although he returned for the playoffs, he wasn't quite the same pitcher he had been earlier in the season. The Cubs didn't have anyone to match up against the Braves' stellar pitching staff of Greg Maddux, John Smoltz, and Tom Glavine. The Braves swept Chicago, but were eventually beaten by the San Diego Padres for the National League pennant.

Sosa finished with a fabulous season. To go with his 66 home runs, the second best ever to McGwire's 70, he led the National League with 158 RBIs and 134 runs scored. Although he still struck out 171 times, he hit .308 and walked 73 times, both career highs. Moreover, he established himself in the minds of everyone who saw him play as perhaps the best all-around player in the game and one of its greatest ambassadors. He may have lost the home run race, but he won something even more important — the hearts of baseball fans everywhere.

Chapter Twelve:
1998

A Hero for the World

After such a spectacular and grueling season, most ballplayers would have gone on a vacation, taking time off and resting. Sosa had been planning to do just that, and then to see the Sammy Sosa Foundation begin construction on a children's hospital in the Dominican Republic. But Hurricane Georges had changed all that.

As soon as the season ended, without a day's rest, Sosa turned his attention to his homeland. The hurricane had left towns isolated from one another, and the basics of human life — food and water — were in short supply. As his friend Bill Chase described it, San Pedro de Macorís "looked like an A-bomb hit it." Through his foundation, Sosa arranged for an immediate shipment of 80,000 pounds of rice, beans, and cooking oil to his hometown.

When baseball fans heard what Sosa was doing, they wanted to thank him for all the enjoyment he had given them during the season. Checks began to pour into the foundation, many of them in the amount of $66, a dollar for every home run he had hit. In just a few weeks, nearly $500,000 poured in. Other groups and organizations collected food, blankets, and other supplies, which the foundation arranged to have delivered to the Dominican Republic.

At a ceremony where the city of Chicago gave Sosa a check for $8,500 to help relief efforts, Sosa summed up his attitude. "I've got to go down to my country and take care of the people there," he said. "They don't have anything. But they do have Sammy Sosa."

For several weeks, Sosa worked tirelessly to raise money, appearing on television talk shows, meeting with corporate sponsors, and raising hundreds of thousands of dollars. Everyone gave something, because they knew that Sosa was leading the campaign.

Sosa's unflagging effort to help his people reminded many baseball fans of Roberto Clemente.

Clemente, a native of Puerto Rico who was a star outfielder for the Pittsburgh Pirates in the 1960s and early 1970s, had demonstrated a similar commitment. At the end of the 1972 season, just after he had cracked his three thousandth major league hit, Clemente had spearheaded efforts to help provide assistance to the people of Nicaragua, who had suffered the ravages of an earthquake. In one of baseball's great tragedies, Clemente died when a supply plane he was on crashed.

Earlier in the year, the Dominican government had planned to give Sosa a big parade when he returned home, celebrating the accomplishments that had made him a national hero. But the hurricane changed that plan, too.

The scheduled thirty-mile parade route was cut short. But despite the chaos in the Dominican Republic, thousands and thousands of Sosa's countrymen still turned out for the more modest parade. Sosa was almost speechless at the tremendous outpouring of affection, and he used the occasion to call for still more aid for his country.

He didn't stop there. He was invited to tour Japan with a team of major league All-Stars and play a series of exhibitions against Japanese professional players. Given his spectacular season, many people expected Sosa to back out of the tour. But he viewed the trip as an opportunity to take his fund-raising efforts worldwide.

He traveled with the team to Japan, and showed the depth of his commitment both to baseball and to his country. Sosa was by far the biggest star on the tour, and Japanese fans responded by filling buckets at every ballpark Sosa played in with money for his relief effort. Sosa was even able to make arrangements with the city of Kobe, which several years before had experienced a devastating earthquake, to make two thousand temporary housing units available for use in the Dominican Republic.

He was just as impressive on the field. In the first at bat of his first game, despite having hardly picked up a baseball bat in weeks, Sosa cracked a home run. After reaching home plate, he demonstrated the same traits that had endeared him to American fans. Before running into the dugout, he paused and bowed to the crowd, a sign of respect in Japan. The fans loved it.

The American squad played seven games against

a Japanese All-Star team, plus an exhibition against the Yomiuri Giants. Sosa was named the Most Valuable Player of the series. He stroked three home runs, thrilling Japanese fans, but also demonstrated that he was more than just a slugger. In one memorable play, Sosa was on second base when one of his teammates lofted a foul fly ball down the right field line. When the Japanese outfielder caught the ball, Sosa tagged up and raced to third base, sliding head-first to beat the throw. Such hard, aggressive play impressed the Japanese fans. Even in a game that didn't really matter, after a long and grueling season, Sammy Sosa was still doing whatever he could to help his team win.

When Sosa returned to the United States after the series, he was named the National League's Most Valuable Player by a wide margin over Mark McGwire. McGwire may have set the home run record, but everyone recognized that it was Sosa who had performed the most valuable service to his team. In 1997, the Cubs had won only 68 games. In 1998 — due primarily to Sosa — they had made the playoffs.

A host of other awards followed, but perhaps

none meant more to Sosa than the one he received in Puerto Rico. He was honored by the Puerto Rican government for both his baseball skills and his humanitarian efforts in the Dominican Republic. Vera Clemente, Roberto Clemente's widow, was present and said, "He's not just a good baseball player, but a great human being."

Those words meant more to Sammy Sosa than any award. As he had once said long ago, he had always wanted to be recognized as a good person first, then as a good baseball player. In 1998, he achieved both his dreams in spectacular fashion.

No one in Chicago, San Pedro de Macorís, or points in between will ever forget his accomplishments. Sammy Sosa, the boy who once shined shoes, is a hero for the world.

Matt Christopher®

Lance Armstrong

Kobe Bryant

Terrell Davis

Julie Foudy

Jeff Gordon

Wayne Gretzky

Ken Griffey Jr.

Mia Hamm

Tony Hawk

Grant Hill

Derek Jeter

Randy Johnson

Michael Jordan

Mario Lemieux

Tara Lipinski

Mark McGwire

Greg Maddux

Hakeem Olajuwon

Alex Rodriguez

Briana Scurry

Sammy Sosa

Venus and Serena Williams

Tiger Woods

Steve Young

The #1
Sports Series
for Kids

Read them all!

- Baseball Flyhawk
- Baseball Pals
- Baseball Turnaround
- The Basket Counts
- Catch That Pass!
- Catcher with a Glass Arm
- Center Court Sting
- Challenge at Second Base
- The Comeback Challenge
- Cool as Ice
- The Counterfeit Tackle
- The Diamond Champs
- Dirt Bike Racer
- Dirt Bike Runaway
- Dive Right In
- Double Play at Short

- Face-Off
- Fairway Phenom
- Football Fugitive
- Football Nightmare
- The Fox Steals Home
- Goalkeeper in Charge
- The Great Quarterback Switch
- Halfback Attack*
- The Hockey Machine
- Ice Magic
- Inline Skater
- Johnny Long Legs
- The Kid Who Only Hit Homers
- Long-Arm Quarterback
- Long Shot for Paul

*Previously published as *Crackerjack Halfback*

All available in paperback from Little, Brown and Company